STONE AGE TO IRON AGE BRITAIN

ANNE
ROONEY

9030 00004 9301 8

Badger Publishing Limited
Oldmeadow Road,
Hardwick Industrial Estate,
King's Lynn PE30 4JJ
Telephone: 01438 791037

www.badgerlearning.co.uk

2 4 6 8 10 9 7 5 3

LONDON BOROUGH OF WANDSWORTH	
9030 00004 9301 8	
Askews & Holts	03-Mar-2016
J936.1 JUNIOR NON-FI	£5.99
	WW15022355

Stone Age to Iron Age Britain ISBN 978-1-78464-064-4

Text: © Anne Rooney 2015
Complete work © Badger Publishing Limited 2015

All rights reserved. No part of this publication may be reproduced, stored in any form or by any means mechanical, electronic, recording or otherwise without the prior permission of the publisher.

The right of Anne Rooney to be identified as author of this work has been asserted by her in accordance with the Copyright, Designs and Patents Act 1988.

Publisher: Susan Ross
Project editor: Paul Rockett
Design: Jo Digby Designs

Picture credits:
akg/Bildarchiv Monheim 13; © Sabena Jane Blackbird/Alamy 17; The British Museum 26; leonello calvetti/Shutterstock 4, 7t; Beaker pot and flint knife found accompanying a burial at Barnwood, Gloucestershire, c.2000 BC, Bronze Age (2000-600 BC)/© Cheltenham Art Gallery & Museums, Gloucestershire, UK/Bridgeman Images 16; Creativemarc/Shutterstock 5tl, 5tr, 5bl; Elenarts/Shutterstock 7b; © English Heritage 14; English Heritage/Mary Evans 23; © Heritage Image Partnership Ltd/Alamy 11; © Doug Houghton/Alamy 10; © Hideo Kurihara/Alamy 19; akg-images/Erich Lessing 28; The Bronze Age, Jackson, Peter (1922-2003)/Private Collection/© Look and Learn/Bridgeman Images 18; Mary Evans Picture Library/Edwin Mullan Collection 27; Museum of Somerset/Wikimedia Commons 20; © The Natural History Museum/Alamy 6; © North Wind Picture Archives/Alamy 21; © PRISMA ARCHIVO/Alamy 5bl; Rufflebrothers 8, 15; © Paul Sampson/Travel/Alamy 12; © Paul Stamper/English Heritage 24; © Skyscan Photolibrary/Alamy 22; CC. Wikimedia Commons cover, 15; © World History Archive/Alamy 30.

Attempts to contact all copyright holders have been made.
If any omitted would care to contact Badger Learning, we will be happy to make appropriate arrangements

Printed by Bell & Bain Ltd, Glasgow

STONE AGE TO IRON AGE BRITAIN

Contents

Vocabulary

Do you know these words? Look them up in a dictionary and then see how they are used in the book.

archaeologists	fossilised
causeways	hoards
communal	molten
evidence	temporary

1. The First People in Britain

People first came to Britain nearly a million years ago. They were not like us: there have been four different types of human living here. Modern humans (homo sapiens) are the only survivors.

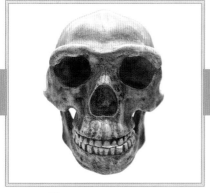

Homo antecessor
Arrived in Britain around 900,000 years ago

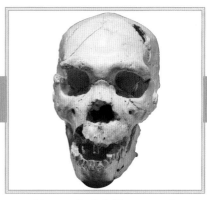

Homo heidelbergensis
Arrived in Britain around 500,000 years ago

Neanderthals
Arrived in Britain around 400,000 years ago

Homo Sapiens
Arrived in Britain around 40,000 years ago

2. The Stone Age

Early humans were hunter-gatherers. They moved around, hunting, fishing, and collecting fruit, berries, nuts and roots to eat.

This was the Stone Age. People made tools like axes and spear-heads from a flaky stone called flint. They chipped bits off the flint to make a sharp edge.

Since people first arrived, there have been several very cold periods, called ice ages. At other times, it was warmer than it is in modern Britain.

When it was cold, humans left Britain – sometimes for thousands of years.

HISTORY HIGHLIGHT!

Can you imagine living through an ice age? The land was covered in thick ice. It would be freezing!

Coming and going

Britain was sometimes joined to Europe by an area of land called Doggerland. During warmer times, melting ice flooded Doggerland and Britain became an island.

When Doggerland was exposed, people could walk from Europe to Britain.

DOGGERLAND

STONE AGE TIMELINE

DATE	EVENTS AND EVIDENCE OF HUMAN LIFE
Around 900,000 BCE	Stone tools have been found that date back to this time. This is the earliest evidence we have of people in Britain.
800,000 BCE	Fossilised footprints found in Norfolk date back to this time
400,000 BCE	A hearth discovered from this period shows us that fire was used
68,000 – 9600 BCE	The last ice age. Sheets of ice on the ground were up to 1.5 km thick!
9600 BCE	People settled permanently
6000 BCE	Doggerland flooded, separating Britain from Europe
4500 BCE	New settlers arrived, bringing farming to Britain
2500 – 2150 BCE	End of the Stone Age

3. Settling Down in the New Stone Age

Hunter-gatherers followed the animals they hunted, making only temporary shelters. But around 4500 BCE, settlers from Europe brought to Britain a new way of living – farming.

Farmers made permanent settlements where they grew wheat and barley. They kept pigs, sheep and cows, and dogs bred from wolves.

They built rectangular houses and large halls from wood or stones.

This is Knap of Howar, in Orkney, a Stone Age house built into the ground.

In the New Stone Age, people dug mines to find flint for tools. They made pottery from clay and used bones from animals they killed to make tools. They carved patterns and made art.

HISTORY HIGHLIGHT!

The New Stone Age is sometimes referred to as the Neolithic Period.
Neo (from Greek 'neos', new) + **lithic** (from 'lithos', stone) = **Neolithic**

This drawing shows a cross-section of Grime's Graves, a New Stone Age flint mine in Norfolk.

Somewhere to live

From about 3000 BCE, people started to make round houses.

Round houses had low walls made of sticks. These were covered in mud that hardened as it dried. The roof was made of dry grass or straw.

Dead and buried

People made tombs from huge upright stones, with slabs across the top. They covered them with soil to make a round mound.

In other places, they built long mounds called barrows, with spaces inside to bury several people. When they were full, the barrows were closed off.

This tomb, Chûn Quoit, in Cornwall, dates from 2400 BCE

Monuments

People also made monuments called henges. A henge is a circular ditch with an earth bank around it. They are only found in Britain and Ireland. The first henges were made around 3300 BCE.

From the Bronze Age, people added stones or wooden posts inside the henge.

Woodhenge, a henge made of wooden posts, in Wiltshire

The most famous henge is Stonehenge in England. It was probably used for religious ceremonies and to keep track of the seasons of the year.

Stonehenge started as a ditch and earth bank around 3000 BCE. The stones were added 500 years later.

HISTORY HIGHLIGHT!

Imagine how hard it would be to cut and move such huge stones using just tools made of bones, stone and wood.

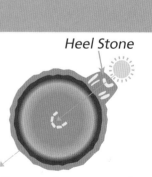

Heel Stone

On Midsummer's Day, someone standing at the centre of Stonehenge would see the sun rise over a stone outside the henge, called the Heel Stone.

4. FROM STONE TO BRONZE

Stone Age people did not use metals. Around 2500 BCE, new settlers arrived who could make things from gold and copper. They brought these skills to Britain.

They were named the Beaker people after the unusual shape of the pottery beakers they used.

Beaker pot, from around 2000 BCE, found in Gloucestershire

Around 2150 BCE, people found out how to make bronze by mixing tin and copper.

Bronze is a much harder metal than copper, so it is better for making weapons and tools.

Bronze slowly took over from stone tools and weapons during the Bronze Age.

Bronze Age axe heads, found in Lincolnshire

Working together

Bronze tools and weapons were made by casting – pouring hot, molten metal into a mould.

People had to work together to mine and cast metals, and to farm.

They dug long ditches to divide the land into areas, and made enclosures to keep animals.

People worked together to make henges. People also worked together to carve a giant white horse into a hillside in Oxfordshire.

Known as the White Horse, it was made by cutting a trench through the grass and soil and filling it with white chalk rock.

HISTORY HIGHLIGHT!

We don't know why the White Horse was carved. The artists might have made it for their gods to look down on, or to mark their territory and warn off enemies. What do you think?

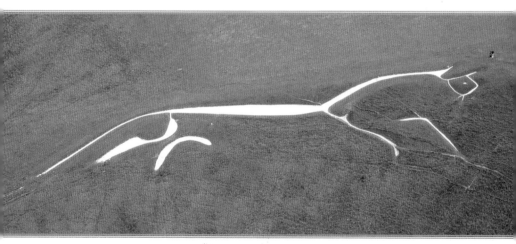

White Horse at Uffington

5. The Iron Age

The Iron Age started around 800 BCE, when people discovered that iron was better for making strong tools and weapons than bronze.

With iron, people made many more tools for farming and building. They made ploughs and sickles, files and nails. It changed how people lived.

This Iron Age sickle was found in Ham Hill, Somerset

The Celts are coming!

Celtic people arrived from Europe in 2000–1200 BCE and again in 500–400 BCE.

They were a war-like people. They used alarming body paint, and collected the heads of people they killed in battle.

The following is a description of Celtic warriors made by the Roman Emperor, Julius Caesar, in 43 BCE:

"All the Britons dye themselves with woad, which produces a blue colour, and makes their appearance in battle more terrible."

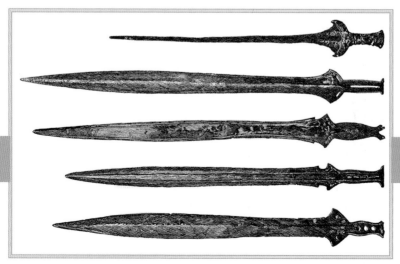

Celtic swords

Everyday life

Most people lived in settlements of several round houses built together.

There was often a hill fort nearby. This was a communal area where people could gather to talk, celebrate and perhaps store crops. It was often on a hill, with a ditch and a fence around it.

This hill in Dorset, known as Maiden Castle, was home to an Iron Age settlement, with houses inside.

Life slowly became more comfortable. People cooked stews and porridge in pots over a fire. They could weave and sew fabric made of wool. They ploughed the fields and planted crops. They made metal coins. By the end of the Iron Age, they even kept chickens.

More than enough

The population was still small – perhaps around a million people. Britons could produce enough metal, food and wool for everyone.

Some goods were traded over long distances and even abroad, to Europe.

To trade, people travelled by boat or using wooden wagons pulled by oxen. Wooden causeways (tracks) made it easier to travel over boggy ground.

Gods and bogs

In Iron Age Britain, druids acted like priests, helping people to worship their gods. People did not go to special places – churches or temples – but worshipped at home and in the fields.

Iron Age people made sacrifices of animals and possibly even humans to their gods.

Iron Age boat discovered at a farm near Peteresborough in Cambridgeshire

25

Sometimes, archaeologists find 'bog bodies'. These bodies have lasted for thousands of years as chemicals in the mud stop them rotting.

Some met violent deaths. They might have been sacrificed, or killed as criminals.

This body was found in a bog in the north west of England. The man died from blows to the top of his head.

The Iron Age ended when the Romans settled in Britain, in 43 CE.

By that time, the Britons were several tribes living in different parts of the country. Sometimes there were fights between tribes.

An interpretation of the Romans arriving in Britain

6. What's left?

People from the Stone Age to the Iron Age left
no written records. What we know about them
comes from the objects they left behind –
including their bodies!

Stone and metal tools have survived, buried
under the ground. We can see the outlines of
settlements, especially looking down from the sky.
And there are monuments, such as Stonehenge
and the White Horse.

In some parts of Britain, people speak older languages than English. The Gaelic spoken in Scotland and the Irish, Welsh and Cornish languages come from the Celts.

Traces of Iron Age fields in Dorset

In the Bronze and Iron Ages, people buried 'hoards' – large collections of valuable objects. They might have been gifts for the gods. But they also left a lot of rubbish around!

We can learn a lot from the way people lived by looking at broken cooking pots and other household items.

HISTORY HIGHLIGHT!

What could future people learn from your rubbish?

Iron Age jewellery found buried in a hoard in Snettisham, Norfolk

Questions

Which type of stone did Stone Age people use to make weapons and tools? *(page 6)*

What was the name of the land that sometimes formed a bridge between Britain and Europe? *(page 8)*

How were round houses made? *(page 12)*

What was a henge? *(page 14)*

Which metals are mixed together to make bronze? *(page 17)*

Name some types of food that Iron Age people ate. *(page 23)*

What are bog bodies? *(page 26)*

Which things can we dig up that tell us about Stone Age, Bronze Age, and Iron Age people? *(page 30)*

Index